History for Kids: History of Religion

Contents

Introduction

Since as far back as humanity could perceive this world and contemplate its own position therein, there has been a deep, primordial need for answers. The curious human mind has always demanded to know why the sun sets, why people die, what comes after, why and when it rains, and so much more. The want of these revelations has usually made people look toward the unreachable – the sky, the underground, the sea, and anywhere else that was suitable for guessing.

What's more, for the majority of human history and for most people, life was always incredibly hard. Food was scarce, nature was unforgiving, and danger lurked around every corner. Even when folks learned how to grow their own food, their farms and crops were still largely at the mercy of nature. Droughts, floods, wildfires, and many other catastrophes would destroy everything. Soon enough, people began to wonder why these things happened to them. Seeing as they had no way of stopping these events, people attempted to interact with these great unseen forces.

We'll never know, but that might be how the first semblances of religion emerged in human populations. Religion has since become one of the central aspects of almost all cultures in the world. For millennia, faith has been the cornerstone of society and civilization, the foundation that supports the structure of life.

Throughout the world, people of different cultures have come up with their own ideas and their own unique ways of interacting with a God or multiple gods. Once upon a time, the most common form of worship was polytheism which simply means a belief in multiple gods as opposed to just one. Civilizations such as the ancient Greeks, Egyptians, Romans, and others believed in hundreds or even thousands of gods. Every important aspect of life had some sort of deity that was in charge. Together, these many gods kept the world in working order and harmony.

Over time, most people left their old religious notions in favor of just one true God, thus paving the way for the rise of monotheism. Today, the two most prevalent religions by far, Christianity and Islam, are both based on the central idea one God. Even though these religions didn't profess that there were individual gods in charge of rivers, winds, war, wisdom, and other things, their one God was still described as having ultimate authority over the entirety of life. And so, folks in the past 2,000 years still prayed for the same things, but they started doing it a little differently.

There have been thousands upon thousands of religions, both big and small, throughout history. This book will be your guide to four of those religions, which are still prevalent today and have left a great impact on the world. As we explore the history and teachings of Christianity, Islam, Buddhism, and Confucianism, we will visit many distinct cultures, all of which have given their own unique approach, not just to faith, but to living on this planet and being human.

Chapter I: The Origins and History of Christianity

Two millennia is a long time, but Christianity is still not that old relative to some other religions in the world. Nonetheless, the time during which Christianity has been on Earth has been eventful, to say the least. The history and destiny of Christianity were also often intertwined with the Jewish religion of Judaism. Along with Islam, Christianity and Judaism also form the trio of Abrahamic religions.

Symbols of the three world religions - Judaism, Christianity and Islam

Christianity originated from a small group of Jews subjugated and persecuted by the Roman Empire. From these humble beginnings, Christianity has grown into the biggest religion in the world, often spread far and wide by people who had very little to do with old Judea (Palestine). For centuries, the Spanish, English, French, and many other seafaring people have spread the faith to virtually every corner of the globe. All of the incredible influence and spread of this powerful message goes back to one humble carpenter.

Jesus of Nazareth and the Founding of Christianity

Christ's Image by Heinrich Hofmann - 19th Century

The recorded story of Jesus is full of hints about the religion's connection to the Jewish faith,

Judaism. Of course, factual records of Jesus' life are fairly scarce. Jesus did exist and preached in 1st-century Judea, then-Roman Empire, present-day Palestine, and Israel. Everything else we know comes from oral tradition and the New Testament's four Gospels. The Gospels were most likely written in the second half of the 1st or in the early 2nd century AD, which wasn't too long after Jesus' death in 30-33 AD.

Either way, Jesus was something of a rebellious figure during his life. Jesus, along with most of his earliest followers, was Jewish. In the course of his life and preaching, he would come into conflict with numerous authorities, particularly those of the Roman Empire, but also powerful religious and political figures among the Jews. By around 26 BC, the ancient Romans had already put present-day Palestine, including Judea, under their control.

Being under Roman rule presented a significant problem for the Jews, who had adhered strictly to Judaism long before the Romans came. Namely, the core of Judaism has always been the belief in one single god, which is Yahweh. The Romans, however, were not only pagans, but they also ascribed divine properties and deified many of their emperors. From the moment when Judea came under Roman control, this fundamental religious disagreement became a source of bitter conflict. The Romans were less than merciful when it came to keeping indigenous religions in check, and they responded to any acts of rebellion with brutal crackdowns.

On top of their strict monotheism, Jewish teachings also spoke of a *messiah,* "the anointed one." According to Jewish beliefs, civilization was put on Earth for a certain period, which ends with the coming of the Messiah, who would essentially be the liberator of the Jewish people. Indeed, this end of mankind's time is apocalyptic but in a way that allows for God's eternal kingdom to arise. During those dark days under the Roman boot, many Jews focused on this concept in the hopes that the Messiah would indeed come and deliver them from their woes.

Jesus wasn't known as Christ from the start. In accordance with Jewish customs, people called him by his name, Jesus, combined with his place of birth or the name of his father. And so, Jesus was known either as Jesus of Nazareth or Jesus, the son of Joseph. "Christ" is more of a title than a name, as it comes from the Greek word "Christos," meaning the same thing that "messiah" means in Hebrew.

Jesus was most likely born somewhere in northern Palestine around the turn of the millennium during the final years of the reign of Herod the Great, who was the king of Judea but a vassal to Rome until his death in 4 BC. Therefore, Christ's rise to prominence, some thirty years later, occurred when Judea was already subjugated under Rome for decades. Jesus' parents were Mary and Joseph, a local carpenter in Nazareth, Galilee. As some Christian teachings suggest, particularly the Gospels of Matthew and Luke, Jesus was the product of an immaculate conception, meaning that Mary came to be pregnant with Jesus and still remained a virgin.

Ancient Palestine Map Printed 1845

During his upbringing in Nazareth, Jesus was most likely educated and taught about various Hebrew

Scriptures, as were many other children of poor Jews in Judea. Jesus was certainly an adherent of Jewish principles found in Judaism, and he preached his wisdom in accordance with the faith. He advocated virtues such as forgiveness and the love of people even if they were enemies. He preached about the noble soul of the poor, the importance of morality, humility, modesty, generosity, solidarity, and much more.

At age 30, John the Baptist, a prominent figure in Christian scripture and an apparent source of inspiration for Jesus and his ministry, baptized Jesus. John was later arrested, and Jesus began to spread the message of an impending Kingdom of God and the end of time. Jesus saw many of his brethren as sinful and straying away from God's light, and he was deeply touched by the suffering of his people. Jesus found the ruling class of wealthy nobles who acquired wealth and power through their association with Roman authorities in Judea particularly sinful.

John the Baptist

Jesus sought for his people to interpret Jewish scripture in a new light and bring themselves closer to God. He preached that the faithful need only confide in their God and stay on the path, and their suffering would be but a transient misfortune. Scripture holds that Jesus performed many miracles during this time, famously magical healing of the sick, walking on water, turning water into wine, and much else. His early followers became more convinced that he was indeed the Messiah, and they saw him as divine. Soon enough, Jesus was the ultimate authority in the people's eyes more so than the establishment in Judea and especially the Roman Empire.

While Jesus' popularity was steadily growing, many still rejected his teachings throughout Galilee in present-day northern Israel. Some were wary of his meddling with the status quo, especially those who profited in their Roman-appointed positions. Others, however, had problems with Jesus on a religious basis, as they considered he was engaging in sacrilege of the Jewish faith.

At one point, most likely after 30 AD, Jesus relocated to Jerusalem to spread his word further.

The religious establishment in Jerusalem, however, had many pro-Roman priests within their ranks. The Romans used the influential religious leaders in Jerusalem to control the Jews of Judea. Jesus quickly came into conflict with these religious figures, and the authorities sought to have him arrested. On the night of the Last Supper, Jesus meet with his closest disciples, and Judas, one of Jesus' disciples, betrayed him.

Mosaic of Last Supper by Giacomo Raffaelli

Pontius Pilate was responsible for deciding Jesus' faith, and he sentenced him to death by crucifixion – a common capital punishment in the Roman Empire.

*Stained Glass Window - Judgment of Jesus Christ by
Pontius Pilate*

As the story goes, people found Jesus' tomb empty
three days after his death, and many reported
seeing him reappear over the next forty days.

Mary Magdalene was the first to see the resurrected Jesus, and she then spread the message to other disciples. People believed God had sent his son, Jesus, down to Earth to fulfill a special task, which was to give his life as an offering toward the redemption of humanity.

The death and resurrection of Christ would become the core of Christian belief, and the man's legacy was immediately strong. The early followers of his message, now called the Church of Christ, continued to cherish his message and meet in secret, doing their best to spread the philosophy. And growing numbers of poor and disenfranchised folks began to listen.

Later History and Important Figures

In the time after Jesus was crucified, the Christians were little more than a Jewish sect mostly operating in secret, and the Romans regarded them as such. Paul of Tarsus (Saint Paul) propelled Jesus' message to new heights. Not only did Saint Paul manage to interest more Jews in Christ's teachings, but he also spread the faith to non-Jews.

St. Paul Statue

Paul and his followers, as well as successors, effectively communicated the message to poor people far and wide. Just like today, many of

Christ's teachings appealed to those whose lives were difficult. A benevolent God who loves us and the idea of an afterlife in the Kingdom of Heaven gave people hope. On top of that, those who simply saw the corruption in the establishment or wanted the Romans gone from their lands also became increasingly likely to listen. Therefore, the hopes that Christ's executioners had of eliminating Christian influence through his death were in vain.

Inclusivity was one particularly strong advantage of Christianity. Judaism had long been reserved for Jews only, while Paul and the other missionaries spread the message of a faith that welcomed all who wished to join. During his life alone, Paul managed to establish Christian churches all over the Roman Empire. Wherever he went, though, the Christian faith met strong resistance from the authorities. Many of the Roman emperors during the early phase of Christianity were brutal in their suppression of the religion. Under some emperors, just being a Christian was illegal, let alone spreading the religion. The sentence was usually death, and it befell many a Christian, giving rise to the concept of martyrdom.

In spite of the persecution, Christianity grew exponentially. After a couple of centuries, the message began to sway some of the powerful people in the Roman Empire. Things took a turn with the rise of one of the most important figures in Christian history – Constantine the Great. After Constantine triumphed over his rivals and seized the Roman throne, he believed that his victory was the work of the Christian God, which led him to convert. This conversion was the turning point for Christians everywhere, and in 325 AD, Constantine proclaimed Christianity the official religion of Rome.

The Holy Cross Appears to Constantine – Painted by Giacinto Gimignani

Christians suffered setbacks under some of Constantine's successors, but there was no turning back the tide at that point. Over the centuries, Christianity flourished and was given many reforms to solidify the faith. The prominence of Christianity also led to much debate over the correct ways of interpreting the scripture and following the religion. The splitting of the Roman Empire into west and east, and the subsequent fall of the Western Empire in 476, gave birth to eastern and western Christianity. The religion was still whole, but it was on a path toward separation. That separation reached its peak with the Great Schism of 1054, when the eastern and western divisions of Christianity became formal, with their seats in Constantinople and Rome, respectively.

Chapter II: All about the Faith

Once you know the background and the origins of Christianity, a lot of other things about the religion are put in perspective. The main teachings and tenets, Christianity's position in the contemporary world, its numerous denominations, and much else about this faith is rooted in that history. In this chapter, we will explore all of these topics and take a closer look at the Christian faith itself.

The Essence of Christianity

The practical purpose of most religions, especially Christianity, is to live your earthly life in a certain fashion. All major religions have certain principles, tenets, or simply teachings that outline life for us. In Christianity, of course, that way of life begins with the Ten Commandments, which almost everyone is familiar with. However, these commandments are far from being the only

Purpose of religion

christianity begyn with 10 commandments

principles that Christians hold dear. Certain variations exist between different Christian denominations, but some principles are universal.

I THOU SHALT HAVE NO OTHER GODS BEFORE ME	VI THOU SHALT NOT KILL
II THOU SHALT NOT MAKE UNTO THEE ANY GRAVEN IMAGE	VII THOU SHALT NOT COMMIT ADULTERY
III THOU SHALT NOT TAKE THE NAME OF THE LORD THY GOD IN VAIN	VIII THOU SHALT NOT STEAL
IV REMEMBER THE SABBATH DAY, TO KEEP IT HOLY	IX THOU SHALT NOT BEAR FALSE WITNESS AGAINST THY NEIGHBOUR
V HONOUR THY FATHER AND THY MOTHER	X THOU SHALT NOT COVET

Core Beliefs

For one, every devout Christian believes that the Bible is the word of God, and Christ was God's son who was sacrificed and died for the sins of humanity. In a way, Christians believe that man is inherently prone to sin. At first, this concept comes across as bleak, but that's far from the truth. First of all, the Bible teaches us that God loves us and has an infinite capacity to forgive. The Christian life is thus a path of redemption and self-improvement. Through true commitment and repentance, no person is beyond redemption. In fact, the very soul of the Christian faith is in the simple belief that even the most sinful among us can find his or her way into the Kingdom of Heaven.

Heaven

A belief in an afterlife is another central piece of the puzzle for Christians. After one's judgment in death, he or she will either end up in Heaven or in Hell. This concept is familiar to most people, and both the Bible and preachers describe these eternal places. Just like Judaism and other religions, the Christian doctrine teaches us that this life is merely the beginning – a transient phase that only serves to decide our outcome in the afterlife. This view of life is very different from that of many other faiths.

The Holy Trinity

*Holy Trinity, by Peter Paul Rubens, Wood Engraving,
Published 1881*

Another crucial and sometimes misunderstood concept is the belief in the Holy Trinity. [The Trinity consists of the God (Father), Son, and the Holy Spirit. These three are not separate and are, in fact, the same. The Trinity simply represents three forms that God has taken, including the original one and his Son, Jesus Christ.] In Christianity, Christ was, in a way, the divine earthly embodiment of God. For this reason, Jesus is often referred to by Christians as God or the Lord. The Holy Spirit is simply God's presence throughout the world to this day.

Trinity

The Bible

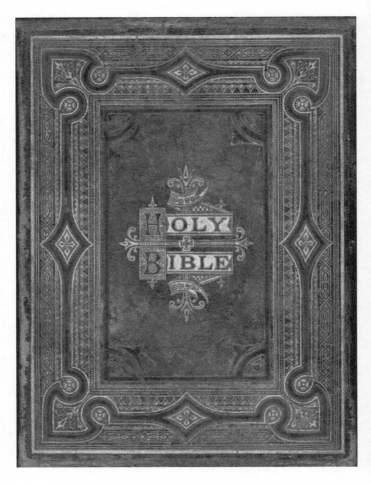

Nineteenth Century Bible Cover

Christians hold the Bible as the word of God. They believe the Bible is the universal truth, as the word of God can never be false. Christians deeply respect the Bible and considered it sacred. This book is not merely prescriptive and filled with instructions, however the Bible is a book of stories and records, many of which carry deep messages and lessons. Some devout Christians spend their lives studying the Bible and contemplating its wisdom.

Holy Sites

Like many other faiths, Christianity has certain holy sites. Apart from places like the Vatican, which is important for Catholics above all, and many renowned cathedrals, churches, and monasteries throughout the world, most Christian holy sites are in present-day Israel.

St Peter's Basilica, at Vatican City

Palace

Jerusalem, as a whole, is one of the holiest sites for Christians] as well as the other two Abrahamic religions. One of the best examples is the place of Jesus' crucifixion on Golgotha just outside of the city. Another important place is the Cenacle, the site of the first Christian church and the believed locale of the Last Supper, where Jesus dined with his disciples before death. Many other important sites are found throughout Israel and Palestine, such as Nazareth, Sepphoris, the Sea of Galilee, and Bethlehem.

The Cenacle (Last Supper Hall), Jerusalem, Israel

Important Art

Needless to say, the Christian religion has spawned untold numbers of magnificent pieces of art, ranging from paintings to sculptures to texts to architecture. People consider certain important structures works of art as a whole, particularly because they include many works of art within them. A perfect example of this is the Sistine Chapel in the Vatican. The walls and the ceiling of this chapel inspire awe in visitors to this day as a great demonstration both of devotion to God and artist Michelangelo's genius. Some of the most famous works by Michelangelo adorn the interior, such as the *Last Judgment* or the *Creation of Adam*. The *Last Supper*, a painting by the famed Leonardo da Vinci, and the *Divine Comedy*, a long narrative poem by Dante Alighieri, are two more examples of revered Christian art.

The Creation of Man from the Ceiling of the Sistine Chapel by Michelangelo

Christianity in Today's World

With a population of some 2.3 billion as of 2015, Christians make up the world's largest religious group by a significant margin. In total, Christianity accounts for almost a third of the total population in the world, which includes the irreligious folks,

Population

36

not just the adherents of existing religions. Just a century ago, the world was home to only 600 million Christians, so the increase has been significant, particularly due to the growth of population. According to the Pew Research Center, the global Christian population is expected to reach close to 3 billion by 2050.

The global Christian population includes Christians of many denominations (as many as 41,000 according to the widest estimates) and degrees of devotion. Even when they are not particularly devout or active, many Christians will still identify with the faith, especially for reasons of culture and heritage.

As of 2010, the ten countries with the largest Christian populations in the world accounted for over a billion of all Christians. The Christians in the USA alone made up more than 11%, while European Christians were about a quarter. In order, Brazil, Mexico, Russia, and the Philippines account for the rest of the top five Christian nations.

Since its start, the Christian faith has affected the world in countless ways and profoundly influenced the course of civilization. As such, this religion has a powerful legacy, which permeates many facets of society, especially communities and family life. The traditional family structure throughout the West and beyond is, in a way, the legacy of Christian values. One of the most striking examples of Christian influence was what happened in the Roman Empire from the 4th century on. Over time, not only did the adherents of the faith grow in numbers throughout the empire but the state itself became Christian.

Many institutions we take for granted today evolved from Christian organizations and communities. For instance, the important Christian principle of charity, as preached by Jesus, gave rise to many hospitals and other care centers, as well as international relief organizations. Christians have also made major contributions to learning institutions throughout the Christian world, which produced many universities that stand to this day.

All in all, Christianity has shaped cultures, mentalities, social structures, and even governments. The relationship between church and state has always been an important topic. During the Middle Ages, the bond between the crown and the faith was crucial to unite people in almost all European countries. Even though we now live in secular societies where the church and state are clearly separated, the historic influence of Christianity in the very foundation of our civilization is indisputable.

Denominations

Christianity has perhaps thousands of different denominations. Like in many other faiths, these denominations are simply different traditions built on the same core principles. The existence of these denominations is complicated and deeply rooted in many historical events. As people moved throughout the world and further from the seat of the religion, new ideas cropped up, and folks came up with their own unique ways of worship that suited them the best.

The three largest denominations of Christianity are Roman Catholic, Eastern Orthodox, and Protestant. This split began with the Great Schism in the 11th century when the Church was split between east and west. Protestantism, along with a number of other denominations, split off from Roman Catholicism in the 16th century. This separation started with Martin Luther's publication of the Ninety-five Theses in 1517 which occurred because of various disagreements in the interpretation of scripture, teaching, and other matters.

Martin Luther

Roman Catholics are still the largest group with major strongholds in Italy, Spain, France, and beyond. In fact, Brazil has the largest Catholic population by far at over 130 million. Overall, more than a billion believers adhere to the Roman Catholic Church, accounting for around half of all Christians.

Protestants are a strong second with around 900 million adherents. Places with a significant Protestant presence are the US, Scandinavia, UK, Germany, and much of sub-Saharan Africa. Unlike Catholicism and Orthodoxy, Protestantism

Protestant [focuses more heavily on theological philosophy than tradition. The Protestants also baptize themselves during adulthood, unlike the Orthodox and Catholic Christians who do this in infancy.] Another important point of difference is that the Protestants don't pray to Mary or consider her holy, even though she was a crucial figure as the mother of Jesus.

Last but certainly not least, there are the Orthodox Christians, adherents of the eastern religion after the Schism. Eastern Orthodoxy accounts for some 260-270 million believers worldwide, particularly in Russia (40%) and a significant part of other Eastern European nations. Orthodoxy is also particularly strong in the Balkans, the influence area of the former Byzantine Empire, in countries such as Greece, Serbia, Romania, and Bulgaria.

Many of the much smaller, often highly localized denominations fall under the wing of these big three either as recognized or unrecognized separations. All told, only around 1% of the world's Christians don't worship under one of the three major denominations. Separations such as these have historically been sources of conflict from time to time, but Christians worldwide see themselves as deeply connected in their faith in Christ and the one Christian God

Chapter III: The Origins and History of Islam

Islam is the youngest religion we will talk about by a significant margin, as it started in the 7th century AD. Nonetheless, this religion has had an impressive history in that it has spread far and has affected our world in many profound ways. Arguably, Islam has been more successful than some religions that preceded it.

This faith can be traced back to Mecca and Medina in the Arabian Peninsula whence it proceeded to reach every corner of the globe. Like Christianity, Islam has seen its share of ups and downs, and it all goes back to one central figure.

The Early Life of Prophet Muhammad

Muhammad, the last of God's prophets and the founder of Islam, was born around 570 AD in

Mecca, in the present-day Kingdom of Saudi Arabia. He was born when many tribes and their leaders fought each other throughout the Arabian Peninsula. We don't know much about Muhammad's formative years, but he was born into the Hashim clan of the Quraysh tribe and most likely grew up as an orphan, raised by Abu Talib, his uncle. This tribe was highly successful in trade and involved in Mecca's political life.

Prophet Muhammad

Muhammad spent most of his early life as a merchant, and he made a name for himself in this business by working for his uncle. His reputation was one of a capable merchant as well as an honest man, as evident by the nickname he earned, "al-

Amin," which means trustworthy. Around age 25, Muhammad had to make his way in the world, and he sought employment with a widowed woman by the name of Khadija. She was a wealthy woman involved in trade, and she needed someone to help her take her goods to Syria.

Muhammad soon became a renowned caravan trader and married Khadija in 595, who gave birth to at least seven daughters and sons in the course of their 25-year marriage. One of Muhammad's daughters, Fatima, married his cousin, Ali ibn Abi Talib (Ali for short), who became an important figure later on. Even though polygamy, or having many wives, was normal in the region then as it is today, Khadija was Muhammad's only wife until she died. After her death, Muhammad remarried to a woman named Sawdah.

According to Islamic tradition, the year 605 was important in Muhammad's life. Namely, the story happened at the Kaaba, the holy place of worship in Mecca. The sacred Black Stone needed replacing in the Kaaba's wall because of ongoing renovations. Putting this stone back in place was seen as a great honor for the one who was given the task. The different clans operating in Mecca all wished that one of their own would be entrusted with the task, which caused disagreement.

Kaaba

Seeing no agreement in sight, the prominent figures of Mecca decided to grant the honor to the first man who entered through the city's gate. In an incredible stroke of luck, that man was Muhammad. The moment when Muhammad picked up the stone and put it back in its place has been immortalized in Islamic tradition. While Muslims are forbidden from creating any visual depictions of Muhammad, other cultures did illustrate the moment. In particular, Muhammad and the clan leaders with the Black Stone can be seen in certain arts produced in Mongol-controlled Persia during the 14th century.

Muhammad continued to be involved in affairs at Mecca and build his name. In a few short years, the history of Islam would officially begin in 610, at least for Muhammad himself.

Islam's Beginnings and History

During Muhammad's time, the tribes of the Arabian Peninsula were scattered, highly mobile, and generally polytheistic, believing in a number of their own unique gods. Even then, the people often gathered in the important religious center of Mecca and worshiped at the Kaaba, just like Muslims do today. People most likely already worshipped Allah at that time.

Muhammad became increasingly devoted to religious life as he got older. He was known to have made pilgrimages and indulged in rituals. According to Islamic teachings, in 610 an angel by the name of Gabriel revealed himself to Muhammad. This turning point happened on Mount Jabal al-Nour, where Muhammad was meditating in a cave during one of his religious pilgrimages.

As Islamic teachings suggest, the angel said to Muhammad, "Recite in the name of your Lord, who creates, creates man from a clot. Recite for your Lord is most generous." These were the words of God, spoken by an angel on behalf of God, and intended to be passed on to humanity by Muhammad, the earthly prophet of God.

The angel instructed Muhammad to recite God's word to the world, and this word would become the Muslim holy book, Quran. Muslims believe that the message was the same message given to God's earlier messengers, as described in the other two Abrahamic religions. Islam also teaches that

Muhammad continued to receive other divine messages for the rest of his years on Earth. Islam teaches Muslims Gabriel did not tell Muhammad the entire Quran when they first met. Instead, the holy book consists of all those messages that Muhammad received after the initial revelation during a period of more than twenty years.

However, the experience unsettled Muhammad, so he kept it secret for a while. Muhammad confided in his wife, Khadija, and his close friend, Abu Bakr, and Islam teaches that Khadija was the first person to believe Muhammad's miraculous story. Muhammad's first reception of Gabriel's message is still one of the points of contention between Sunnis and Shias, the two main sects of Islam. Shias, who are a minority sect, believe that Muhammad was neither frightened nor disturbed. They believe that he was joyous and happy to spread God's message right from the start.

Around the year 613, Muhammad began to preach and spread the message in mostly in Mecca but also beyond. The period between the revelation and the start of Muhammad's preaching activity is called "fatra." Muhammad taught then what Islam teaches today, most importantly that there is no other god but Allah, and people should devote themselves to his way. Apart from monotheism, Muhammad preached to the nonbelievers that they would meet a terrible punishment once the end came.

In general, the people of Mecca, especially those who were rich and powerful, rejected with ridicule the things that Muhammad preached. Nonetheless, he did manage to acquire a relatively small following, especially since he wasn't persecuted early on. Over time, the evolving message that Muhammad brought forth began to clash with more important aspects of life and worship in Mecca.

The worship of idols and a belief in multiple gods were important principles in Mecca, and once Muhammad began to preach against these things, trouble was on the horizon. Even Muhammad's own tribe disapproved of his ways, but still, Muhammad didn't come under direct attack. Instead, Mecca's prominent figures essentially tried to pay Muhammad to abandon his efforts or leave the city.

Over time, pressure began to build, and Muhammad found himself very unwelcome. This trouble led to one of the most important events in Islamic history, which was Muhammad's move from Mecca to Medina in 622. This event is known as Hegira, or Hijra, marking the point when the Islamic calendar begins.

Mohammed riding a camel during an event known as the Hijra

Upon arrival, Muhammad found the city of Medina in strife among local interest groups. He quickly got involved and brought an end to this conflict, later solidifying his position in the city and making a base out of it. Muhammad grew more influential and powerful and had a hand in the reforms and restructuring of Medina. He helped draft a constitution and establish a system of peaceful relations between his Muslims and the other communities in the region. Still, many folks chose to convert to Islam and join him. Soon enough, the first Islamic state emerged around Medina.

Years of conflict ensued between Muhammad and the rulers at Mecca. Muhammad was victorious on numerous occasions, such as in the Battle of Badr, but he also suffered losses, such as the Battle of Uhud in 625. In the end, though, Muhammad headed an army of some 10,000 Muslim followers, which was enough to overwhelm the city of Mecca. Muhammad established control over the city around 627 and his followership grew. In the course of the next couple of years, virtually all tribes in Arabia submitted to the new way. With the unification complete, Muhammad put together a major Muslim pilgrimage in 632, which is called the "Farewell Pilgrimage." Muhammad passed away in 632.

Muhammad's legacy was immense right from the start, and the time after his death would be a period of major expansion for Islam. Muhammad's succession is now another source of disagreement between the two Muslim sects. According to the majority Sunni sect, Muhammad was succeeded by his friend and confidant Abu Bakr. Not everyone agreed with this, however, and a portion of Muhammad's Muslims went to his cousin Ali. This splinter movement would later become the Shia sect of Islam.

Muhammad left behind a system of governance, among many other things. Islamic leaders were known as caliphs whose dominion was called a caliphate. Some of the caliphates who followed over the centuries would turn into some of the greatest empires this world had known. The early empires brought about the Islamic Golden Age and changed the world forever.

Already during the first four successors of Muhammad, Islam spread throughout the Middle East. The Arabs conquered North Africa as well, and the successors of the early caliphates would spread into Europe. One of the greatest empires that would emerge from Muhammad's legacy was the Ottoman Empire.

Chapter IV: The World's Second Largest Religion

As the world's second largest religion, Islam brings under its wing some 1.8 billion Muslims, which is close to a quarter of the world's total population. According to numerous sources and research papers, Islam is also the fastest growing religion in the world. As before, this chapter will explore some of the most important teachings and principles of the religion as well as Islam's position and influence in the modern world.

The Essence of Islam

Being an Abrahamic religion like Christianity and Judaism, Islam rests on the notion of only one God, who Muslims refer to as Allah. Allah is very much like the Christian God, so much so, that his name is little more than a translation into Arabic. Allah is the creator and overseer of everything. He is omniscient and omnipotent; Allah is invisible, can't be heard; Allah judges and punishes the deserving but is merciful and fair. The one major difference between Allah and the Christian God is that Allah has no children.

The Quran

Holy book

The central piece of scripture in Islam, the Quran, is the direct word of God much like the Bible is for Christians. Allah spoke the word through his earthly prophet, Muhammad. The text consists of 114 parts, which are known as the "suras." The Quran details all facets of life and society, giving instructions for how Muslim people and communities should live and practice their faith. Apart from the Quran, Muslims also use the Hadiths, a collection of things that the prophet Muhammad said during his life, for guidance in their lives.

Core Teachings

Condensing the philosophy of an entire religion into a few central teachings or tenets is difficult, but there are ways to summarize. What greatly helps in this task is the fact that Muslims all over the world mostly live in agreement when it comes to the interpretation of scripture and the way of worship.

One important aspect consists of the six articles, or axioms, of faith, together known as the concept of Iman. These beliefs are universal to all Muslims. The first and most important is the belief in one god, Allah. One of the greatest transgressions a Muslim can commit is the belief in or worship of any other god. Second is the belief in angels, which states that there are angels all around us, created by Allah to watch over us and mind what we do.

Muslims also believe strongly in prophets, which is the third article of faith. While Muhammad is the most important one, others were throughout the world, most of which the scriptures of the other Abrahamic religions name. As the fourth article, Muslims believe in the holiness of other Abrahamic scriptures like the Torah or the Christian Psalms and Gospels. The reason that the Quran is more important and revered is that

Muslims believe this was the last godly word given to humanity while people distorted the earlier scriptures over time.

For the last two articles of faith, Muslims believe in Judgment Day and destiny. Just like Christians, Muslims believe that the world will end one day. On that day, Allah will descend from Heaven to judge us all and decide, with fairness and mercy, who will go to Heaven and who will go to Hell. This idea is similar to the Christian concept of Rapture. The belief in fate or destiny, however, simply states that God already knows everything we will do. In Islam, God's knowledge of the future isn't at odds with free will.

The Five Pillars

The Five Pillars of Islam are another great way to summarize the essence of the faith. These principles concern worship or, more precisely, the way in which a Muslim should practice his or her faith. The first pillar, which is also the first step for all newcomers to the religion, is the declaration of faith. This declaration is an acknowledgment of belief in the one true God and his earthly prophet, Muhammad.

The second pillar of Islam is daily prayer, which Muslims engage in five times a day.

The third pillar, also called Zakah, denotes the importance of charity and kindness. In general, Muslim doctrine doesn't look down on wealth like many Christian teachings do. However, Islam states that wealth is a responsibility as much as a blessing, which means that the rich are blessed by helping the poor.

The fourth pillar is the Ramadan, a well-known Muslim month of fasting. Every year during the month of Ramadan, Muslims are not to eat, drink, or engage in sexual activity between sunrise and sunset. Prayer and worship take a front seat before everything else during this holy month.

Last but not least, the fifth pillar is the Hajj pilgrimage. This principle urges every capable, adult Muslim to undertake a pilgrimage to the holy site in Mecca at least once in their life.

Holy Sites

Muslims consider many places in the world sacred, and most of them are in the Middle East. The aforementioned Mecca (Saudi Arabia) is home to the most important location in all of Islam, which is the Kaaba shrine. This famous place is where many Muslims congregate, and Muslims believe Abraham built it around a particular black stone. The biggest reason that Mecca is so important is that Muhammad himself named the city as holy.

Another place that's invaluable to the Muslim faith is Medina, also in Saudi Arabia. Medina is important because it's the resting place of Muhammad, who was buried at the Prophet's Mosque in the center of the city. Muslims also ascribe great importance to Jerusalem because it was the center of their faith before Mecca, as well as the place where Muhammad is believed to have ascended into Heaven at one point.

Mosque of the Prophet Muhammad. Prophet's tomb is under the green dome.

Important Figures

Apart from the people we mentioned in the previous chapter, Islam gives great importance to many of the figures from Judaism and Christianity. Muslims consider Adam, Abraham, Moses, David, and Jesus to have been Allah's prophets, although Muhammad was the last and most important one. Apart from their role, the names are also different in Islamic teachings and they are, respectively, Adam, Ibrahim, Musa, Dawud, and Isa.

Islam in Our World

Although the Middle East has been the historical heartland of Islam, the biggest populations of Muslims today are found in the Asia-Pacific region. The country with the most Muslims is Indonesia with around 230 million believers, although a close second is Pakistan with around 200 million. Although Muslims are by far a minority in India, this country has the third largest Muslim population in the world at around 190 million.

Much of the Muslim world today is comprised of some of the most devout religious folks in the world. By large, major Muslim populations live in strict accordance with their faith, and many Muslim countries still base their legal system on Islamic Law, otherwise known as Sharia. Some Muslim countries such as Turkey, however, embraced secularism during the 20th century.

Before and during Islam's expansion in the course of the Rashidun, Umayyad, and Abbasid Caliphates, Islam influenced the world on a great scale. The Islamic Golden Age saw Muslim cultures absorbing a lot of knowledge from other civilizations and improving upon that wisdom. The Abbasids, for instance, engaged in thorough translation of important works from Greece, Persia, and India. The accumulated knowledge paved the way for prominent learning institutions, and the Islamic world engaged in developing its own science and humanities.

For example, mathematicians, such as al-Khwarizmi, gave us algebra, the evidence rooted in the word itself, "al-jabr." Arabic numerals, which came to Europe by the 13th century and replaced Roman numbers, also revolutionized mathematics.

Statue of Muhammad ibn Musa al-Khwarizmi - famous scientist born in Khiva in 783.

The Islamic world also spread its influence in things like arts and architecture far and wide and also introduced the world to many inventions that affect the world to this day. Already in the 10th century, Qasim al Zahrawi introduced revolutionary surgical tools like the scalpel. Surgery had existed for millennia beforehand, but these tools changed the practice forever. The Muslims also taught us the art of coffee drinking, as they were the first to grind up the beans and boil them in the 15th century. These are only some of the ways in which the Islamic world influenced Western civilization and far beyond it.

Denominations

Islam enjoys great uniformity, but it's not without its splits. Generally, the adherents of Islam in our world are divided into two main branches (sects), which are Sunni Muslims and Shia Muslims.

The first sect gets its name from the Arabic word "sunnah," which roughly translates as "tradition." As such, a Sunni person is simply one that adheres to tradition. Sunni Islam is observed by between 80 and 90% of all Muslims worldwide. In addition, Sunni Islam has four major schools of thought, also known as Madhhabs. These include the Hanafi, Shafi, Maliki, and the Hanbali Madhhab, each predominant in its respective regions of the Sunni world.

The schools are definitely not sects, and the differences aren't very big, as they mostly revolve around the interpretation of scripture. Many Sunni

Muslims view themselves as the only true followers of Islam, and the disagreements between the Shia and Sunni interpretations have been the object of scholarly debate for centuries.

The Shias, otherwise known as Shi'ites, account for up to 15% of all Muslims worldwide. Their largest concentrations are in Iran and Iraq, and they are much represented in Lebanon. However, Shia minorities exist throughout the Muslim world. Shia Islam, too, has sprouted a few different branches over the centuries, the most prominent are the Twelvers, Ismailis, and Zaidis.

Although they are a tiny minority, other sects of Islam exist outside of the two main branches. A particularly (in) famous example in the West is America's Nation of Islam. Wallace Fard Muhammad founded this religion and political movement in 1930s Detroit, Michigan. He claimed to be an incarnation of Allah and proclaimed African-Americans as the chosen one while believing white Americans to be devils. Although the Nation of Islam has had prominent members in their time, one example being Malcolm X, it has never garnered any wider support and many label is as a hate group. Mainstream Islamic scholars across the board don't recognize the NOI or any other such group as legitimate.

Chapter V: The Origins and History of Buddhism

As far as major, relevant religions go, Buddhism is old by all standards, though still not the oldest. 2,500 years is a very long time, and it makes this religion older than the Roman Empire, for instance, yet its age is still dwarfed by the likes of Hinduism, which goes more than 4,000 years back if all the Hindu and Vedic traditions are taken into account. As we proceed, you will also learn a bit about Hinduism, as Buddhism shares some things with this religion of the Indian subcontinent. As always, however, it all begins with one man and his vision.

Siddhartha Gautama

Much like Jesus Christ, the Buddha (Siddhartha Gautama) was a spiritual and contemplating man who sought to challenge the status quo in many ways and give folks a new perspective on life.

Unlike Jesus, however, Siddhartha didn't have humble beginnings, as he was born to the noble Gautama family of the Shakya clan in northern India – Lumbini, present-day Nepal. The exact time when Siddhartha was born is unknown, but it was likely sometime in the 5th century BC, passing away between 410 and 370 BC. Buddhist traditions put his birth closer to 563 BC, however, and both historians and Buddhist scholars agree that he lived around eighty years.

Buddha

Within the ancient Indian caste hierarchy, Siddhartha's clan was a part of the warrior-ruler caste. Needless to say, Siddhartha's life was one of abundance right from the start with no shortage of

74

luxury. Siddhartha was born and grew up was a relatively unstable and uncertain era. Numerous states, such as the one ruled by Siddhartha's clan, were highly competitive. This period was also one of emerging philosophies and schools of thought, many of which sought to question the religious status quo in India. This religious order revolved mostly around ancient Vedic traditions, and a growing number of people began to feel that these teachings weren't working for them.

Indeed, this time was one of great misfortune for many people in India. Poverty and suffering were rampant. The people were eager for any kind of relief, but this relief didn't seem to come from the religious establishment anymore. These circumstances left an empty space that needed to be filled with fresh, profound philosophies to get the people back on track. And that's how many philosophies of the day, including the one of Siddhartha Gautama, started rising to prominence.

Traditions state that from an early age, his father and family sheltered the Buddha from worldly suffering. Despite his parents' care, young Siddhartha never ceased showing interest in the outside world. In fact, he was drawn to the world, and his life of nobility seemed to interest him very little. One of the key moments in Siddhartha's life came in his early adulthood when he once snuck out of his palace.

Siddhartha walked the land and beheld the world, noticing that life was full of suffering. People and animals alike lived a harsh existence, withered, and died. Not only did Siddhartha take note of these hardships, but such existence illustrated that life was fundamentally transient.

At this time, Siddhartha had already been given a life and a role to play. He was married, had a son, and was destined for great things. Nonetheless, Siddhartha decided to abandon this life and disappear into the world. Siddhartha Gautama went on a path of meditation, learning, and, above all, asceticism. Asceticism is a regimen of strict self-discipline and self-deprivation. All indulgence is absent for the purpose of fostering spirituality over the body.

The young Buddha lived a miserable existence, but his pursuit was one of enlightenment. Faced with such seemingly meaningless suffering all around him, he wanted to find a deeper meaning in life and answers to other existential questions. The life of the ascetic at that time had much to do with earlier Indian traditions, many of which can be found in Hinduism. During Siddhartha's time, devout Hindus commonly deprived themselves with the goal of freeing their soul, known in Sanskrit as "atman."

At some point on his painful journey, Siddhartha became aware that there was no enlightenment found yet. A stranger's mercy in the form of food when he felt the lowest brought another idea to his head. He began to realize that his ascetic ways were doing little more than adding to the world's suffering, of which there was already too much. Siddhartha devised something known as the Middle Way.

This path toward enlightenment was the perfect, flawless balance between total self-deprivation and over-indulgence, later evolving into the Noble Eightfold Path, which is one of the core concepts of Buddhism. A person must walk this path in order to achieve true enlightenment, as the Buddha managed to do during his life.

Buddhism's Founding and History

According to Buddhist tradition, Siddhartha's enlightenment and the de facto birth of Buddhism began shortly after the Buddha came up with the Middle Way. As the story goes, Siddhartha sat under a Bodhi tree in deep contemplation, thinking about his journey up to that point and his idea of the Middle Way.

Siddhartha decided that this was the perfect spot to engage in his greatest attempt at meditation yet. For days, Siddhartha would meditate with intense focus, with nothing but final enlightenment on his mind. He finally reached nirvana, the state of total enlightenment, bliss, and liberation, and the Middle Way became clear as day in his mind. He realized that the path toward true liberation from suffering lay in the balance between mind and body. Siddhartha had now become the Buddha, the "enlightened one."

For context's sake, the concept of constant rebirth, "samsara," is a deeply embedded idea in Vedic and Hindu teachings. This concept is a cycle of death and rebirth that causes suffering and keeps people trapped, and to liberate one's self from this cycle is the goal in life. Buddha's idea of that liberation was the concept of nirvana, achieved through committed meditation and adherence to the Middle Way.

Upon attaining enlightenment, the Buddha decided that it was time to spread the word of his incredible experience to others, as he was confident that he had found the end to suffering. According to Buddhist tradition, this occurred around 528 BC. The Buddha proceeded to spend more than forty years spreading his wisdom and showing people the way. More and more folks began to listen and join his path, and he crossed great distances all over India on foot.

By the time the Buddha passed away, around 483 BC according to tradition, a significant number of spiritual teachers had adopted his teachings. These teachings were slowly molded into a religion by the Buddha's followers, and they established a firm foothold in central parts of India. Temples began to crop up throughout the land, and the ruling classes took notice of the emerging religion.

This time was one of the Maurya Empire in India and, in the 3rd century BC, the Ashoka the Great ruled the empire. He looked kindly upon Buddhism and saw to it that Buddhism be instated as the state religion in his country. These changes provided an incredible boost to Buddhism, which could now be solidified and spread throughout the Indian Subcontinent thanks to state resources. In a couple of centuries, Buddhism had spread well beyond India.

Buddhism and India, in general, suffered a significant setback in the 6th century AD, when the country was sacked by the invading Huns. The invaders had little regard for the Buddha's teachings, and they destroyed a great number of temples. The Huns were later defeated, though, and Buddhism was back on track. Throughout these centuries, Buddhism underwent many reforms and additions by different religious circles. Even though it became a prominent aspect of life in India, it was split into different schools of thought. Because of these splits, schools like the Mahayana, Theravada, Vajrayana, and Tibetan Buddhism came to exist.

Through history, Buddhism has had a pan-Buddhist consciousness, so to speak. Monastic communities from different traditions would come together many times throughout history to deliberate and initiate reforms. These events would be known as Buddhist Councils, with six of them occurring by 1954. As tradition states, after Siddhartha Gautama's death his follower and disciple Mahakashyapa received an important task to compile the teachings and provide one whole doctrine that would help spread Buddhism in the future. The First Council was thus held at Rajagriha around the end of the 5th century BC.

Overall, despite the splits and the many changes in Indian society and governance through the centuries, Buddhism remained strong and important. In the 13th century, its position began to weaken in India, largely due to Islamic invasions from the Middle East but also because of domestic issues. In the course of the 13th century, Buddhism all but vanished from India.

Luckily by this time, the religion had spread far beyond, and its footholds in China, Japan, Korea, Tibet, and much of Southeast Asia ensured the survival, along with its great diversity of schools and traditions. Buddhism reached as far north as Mongolia during the 16th century, and the ideas had certainly made their way further than that as well. Another challenge for Buddhism came with the rise of communist regimes in Asia during the 20th century. The communists were often very intolerant of these traditions, and Buddhists have endured numerous crackdowns throughout the continent toward the second half of the 20th century.

Chapter VI: The Buddha's Wisdom

Buddhism is one of the more diverse religions. Owing to its traditionally tolerant ways along with expansion, Buddhism has picked up different ideas along the way and sprouted many branches and schools of thought. Although it has traditionally been an almost exclusively Asian tradition, Buddhism has reached most parts of the world, and up to 500 million people practice various forms of the religion. *Population*

The Essence of Buddhism

do they believe in anything Buddhism is essentially atheistic, meaning that Buddhists don't believe in any god, at least not in the Christian or Muslim sense. The Buddha himself is seen as an ideal or someone to emulate, but he is given no divine properties. More revered than the man himself is the entirety of his teaching, way of life, and wisdom, all of which can perhaps best be summarized as *"dharma."* Dharma is a Sanskrit word used to simply encapsulate the entirety of these teachings and all the core principles the Buddha left behind.

The Four Noble Truths

The Four Truths essentially outline the Buddhist worldview, and accepting these truths and being aware of them at all times is central to being a Buddhist. The first of the truths of life is that there is suffering, referred to as "dukkha." Buddhists view that life is essentially suffering and not just for us humans. The world itself revolves around suffering. Everything withers and dies, all earthly creatures suffer pain, and humans especially are prone to an incredibly wide range of psychological suffering.

The Second Noble Truth is "samudaya." This truth states that all suffering has an underlying cause, which is in our inherent need to crave, need, and attach ourselves to this world. Detachment from this world is one of the core principles of

Buddhism, as those who strive toward Buddhahood must disconnect themselves from both the good and the bad in life.

Thirdly, "nirodha," teaches us that there is an end to our suffering. Despite life's harshness, every one of us has the capacity to end the suffering in life and achieve true contentment. As the Fourth Noble Truth states, this salvation is the Noble Eightfold Path, which will lead us to happiness if we follow it diligently.

Buddha and the Noble Eightfold Path

The Three Jewels and the Three Marks of Existence

(handwritten margin note: refuge from what)

Another important aspect of the Buddhist philosophy is found in the Three Jewels, which are beliefs in which a Buddhist is supposed to find refuge. The first of the Jewels is the "belief" in the Buddha or, more precisely, his path and his wisdom. The second belief is the one in dharma, comprising the entirety of the Buddha's wisdom. The third concerns the sangha, one's Buddhist community, be it a temple or some other form of congregation.

Sensoji Temple, the oldest temple in Tokyo

The Three Marks of Existence are another way for Buddhists to explain life. The first mark, again, is dukkha and the acceptance of inherent suffering that comes with life. "Anicca," or impermanence, is the second concept. Everything in this world, be it physical or mental, is constantly changing – nothing ever lasts. The third mark of our existence is the non-existence of "anatta," or the soul. Unlike the Hindus, Christians, and many others, Buddhists don't believe that humans or any living beings have a soul. Instead, Buddhists believe in karma.

Karma

Karma is an often misunderstood concept. More than being a concept of divine retribution or justice, karma is basically a system of cause and effect. This concept is different from what we in the West mean when we use the word "karma" colloquially. In essence, there are good, bad, and neutral karmas in Buddhism. Buddhists accumulate good karma through kind and righteous conduct but also through things like meditation. The concept is like that of Hindu karma. Karma is accumulated through our actions in life, and it affects our circumstances in the next life, which brings us to another crucial concept that Hindus and Buddhists share.

The Cycle of Rebirth

The cycle of rebirth, also known as "samsara," is the familiar concept of reincarnation. The cycle of rebirth is rather specific and well-detailed in Buddhist philosophy as well. Buddhists believe that each person must go through many rebirths, each time into one of the six main realms. These realms are separated into three good and three harsh realms. The good realms are those of gods, demigods, and humans. The realms of misfortune are those of animals, ghosts, and hell. Karma is what drives the process and determines not only which realm the Buddhist ends up in after rebirth, but also his or her circumstances once in that realm. Although the human realm itself is full of suffering, its main advantage is that humans are given an opportunity to attain nirvana or

90

enlightenment, which marks liberation and a final end to suffering.

The Noble Eightfold Path

The Noble Eightfold Path, sometimes called the Middle Way, was the path that the Buddha walked toward his enlightenment and final liberation. This path is the one that every Buddhist must walk to attain nirvana. Simply put, it is the Buddhist way of life, and it covers the Buddhist religious practice and spiritual life.

The path is comprised of eight core concepts that must be adhered to, and they are, in turn, divided among three aspects of Buddhist conduct. The first group concerns wisdom, which is "prajna." The two principles are Right Understanding and Right Thinking. These two focus on the understanding of the Four Noble Truths and a liberation-oriented mindset.

The second category, "shila,"consists of three tenets that denote morality and virtuous conduct. Right Speech governs a Buddhist's use of the gift of language. The power to speak is given great importance in Buddhism, and using this blessing to spread gossip, curse people, engage in meaningless talk, or tell lies is the antithesis of Buddhist conduct. Buddhists value silence in the absence of valuable things to say. Right Conduct is exactly as it sounds, revolving around the Five Precepts, which we will cover soon. The last of the three is Right Livelihood, which instructs the Buddha's followers to make their living via honest means and through work that isn't at odds with the Five Precepts in general.

"Samadhi," which is concentration and meditation, encapsulates the last three steps on the path. Right Effort (in thought) instructs the Buddhist to mind the contents of his or her head. A Buddhist must make every effort to weed out ill will or other negative thoughts and cherish the good. Right Mindfulness means a Buddhist exercises and cherishes a constant awareness of his or her feelings, thoughts, body, and mind meaning self-awareness and self-control. Finally, Right

Concentration focuses on meditation. Meditation is the cornerstone of Buddhist practice, and Right Concentration means that one should make it his or her life's mission to achieve enlightenment through meditation. That also means doing it right and meditating in a way that was prescribed by the Buddha. The practice of meditation and many other aspects of the path can vary between different schools of thought.

Samadhi Buddha Statue at Anuradhapura Sri Lanka

Nirvana

So, what is nirvana, or Buddhist enlightenment? Simply put, nirvana or nibbana is a state achieved through years of meditation and searching, which liberates one from attachment and thus suffering – it is bliss. Buddha was the first to achieve this state, and Buddhists strive to emulate that. An important way in which nirvana breaks one's dukkha is the cessation of samsara that ensues. Stopping the cycle of rebirth is the ultimate goal of Buddhism, and it's also an important concept in Hinduism.

The Five Precepts

The Five Precepts can perhaps be viewed as the Buddhist version of the Commandments but then again not exactly because of the concept of karma. The Precepts are more advisory than instructive. The first precept is to never kill or harm other living things, which includes animals in many Buddhist traditions. Indeed, many Buddhists are vegetarians.

The second and third precepts are very straightforward: do not steal and do not lie. Different Buddhist schools might expand or narrow down the exact range of these transgressions, but the core idea is the same.

The fourth precept instructs one not to misuse sex. Among different traditions and especially different levels of practice within those traditions, the definition of this precept can vary. Buddhist monks or nuns, for instance, are generally required to be celibate, which means abstaining from sexual activity altogether. For the general population, the misuse of sex primarily concerns adultery or sexual assault and exploitation.

Buddhist Monks

The fifth precept condemns the use of alcohol or drugs. As you have gathered by this point, Buddhism is all about the clarity of mind, and influencing the mind with psychoactive substances is severely frowned upon.

Throughout the Buddhist world, many ordained personnel at monasteries and other similar communities are subject to five additional precepts. For one, monks are not to eat outside of specifically designated mealtimes. Secondly, dancing and music are to be avoided. The third precept forbids monks from adorning themselves with jewelry, hairstyles, special apparel, and perfumes. Buddhist monks are also not to sit on high positions and, finally, they may not accept gold or silver as charity or any other sort of gift.

Important Texts

As far as scripture goes, one of the most important pieces in Buddhism is the Pali Canon, also known as the Tripitaka. This old piece of writing is huge, taking up close to forty volumes in English. The Pali Canon is a collection of Buddha's teachings and parables that used to be passed down via oral tradition before they were written down for future generations. The Pali Canon is divided into three sections, which are also known as the three baskets of wisdom. These are the Discipline, Teaching, and Higher Doctrine Baskets.

One page of 'the biggest book in the world' (marble slabs inscribed with texts of the Buddhist Tripitaka) at Kuthodaw Pagoda, Mandalay.

Buddhism and Its Schools in Today's World

Buddhism has the strongest foothold in East and Southeast Asia. China has the single largest Buddhist population with over 240 million adherents, even though Buddhists only account for 18% of the total population. Countries with significant Buddhist populations that account for the majority of the people include Cambodia, Thailand, Myanmar (Burma), and Sri Lanka. Despite having its own native faith of Shintoism, Japan is home to a significant concentration of Buddhists as well, making up more than a third of the country with over 45 million adherents.

Buddhism shaped the culture and tradition in every place where people practice it. The religion has contributed to practices such as yoga, meditation, and other spiritual exercises leading Buddhism to become popular well beyond its native regions, and is generally on the rise throughout the world, particularly in the West. Because it reached so many locations and was adaptable, Buddhism has given rise to many well-known schools of thought. These include Theravada, Mahayana, Vajrayana, and Zen Buddhism. Many variations exist among these traditions, especially on the practical side of things, but they all teach their adherents to strive toward Buddhahood.

Chapter VII: The Origins and History of Confucianism

Confucianism, also known as Ruism or the School of Literati, is often called a religion, but it can also be viewed as a philosophy, a method of rule, or a way of life for the person. Europeans visiting China in the 19th century most likely gave this philosophy its name. They might have used the word to describe a range of non-Christian, Chinese philosophies and traditions. Be that as it may, the name is based on Confucius, also known as Kongzi, an ancient Chinese philosopher and scholar who lived between 551 and 479 BC.

Stone Statue of Confucius

Confucius would rise to become one of the most influential intellectuals and philosophers in ancient China and, eventually, well beyond the country. Kongzi emphasized the importance of ancient Chinese traditions, and he strove to push his people to return to these traditions by giving them a fresh perspective, so to speak. Respect for one's parents and elders, or filial piety, the importance of ancestors, and virtuous life – these were the principles Confucius laid down as a way to revitalize contemporary Chinese society.

Confucius and Early Philosophy

Being such an ancient figure, the factual records and specifics of Confucius' life are somewhat difficult to come by. Nonetheless, he was an outspoken teacher and writer, and he had many faithful followers, so we do know quite a bit, both factual and legendary.

Confucius was most likely born in 551 BC, in the then-state of Lu, which is present-day Shandong in the East China coastal region. Kongzi was brought up in an era of instability and contention in China. This instability manifested in philosophical disagreements between different schools of thought, but it would also materialize as political conflict, which culminated with the beginning of the Warring States period of Chinese history around 475 BC. Still, the ongoing clash of philosophies during Confucius' life was a good thing for the development of new ideas. In fact, so many intellectuals and teachers were trying to assert their wisdom between the 6th and 3rd century BC that this period is known as the Hundred Schools of Thought.

From early on, Confucius' young and hungry mind made him eager to give his own two cents to the public. He was raised in the city of Qufu, where he spent a part of his life in the employ of the prince of his state. Confucius worked in different administrative capacities and while honing his philosophies. After that, he proceeded to travel the Chinese lands, which were comprised of many separate states at that time. Confucius' idea was to get employed in as many administrative positions as possible in these different states and advise their governments. Confucius perhaps hoped to spread his philosophy throughout China in this way and spark a wide wave of reforms.

He didn't see himself as an inventor or innovator. He merely sought to revive the good aspects of ancient Chinese traditions and revitalize the virtues of his people. In effect, he saw himself as little more than a reformist. Confucius believed that

Chinese society had strayed from the proper path, and it was his task to reverse that trend. He believed that the solutions to the social unrest and instability of the day were found in religious and moral teachings dating back to the ancient Zhou Dynasty. This dynasty ruled a considerable patch of land in eastern China roughly between 1050 and 770 BC.

Confucius saw that era as a sort of golden age and strongly believed that Chinese civilization should strive to rediscover and reintroduce the morals of the era. Confucius' ideal was a society of honorable, honest men and virtuous women where all individuals would conduct themselves with courtesy and interact according to a well-defined system of relationships, with focus on the respect of one's elders.

Confucius believed that the state should be benevolent and kind to its subjects while, in turn, the citizens cherished loyalty, duty, and respect for authority. The goal was to build a society that lived and functioned in total harmony not just with itself but also with all that is divine and above humanity. By extension, every person would be at harmony with him or herself while also maintaining the same relationship with the divine. While he still maintained all this was merely a reintroduction of the ways of old, many modern scholars believe that Confucius was a revolutionary teacher.

His travels brought him little success in the way of getting rulers to implement his values in any meaningful degree. Toward the later part of his life, Confucius decided to go back home and open his own school that would be available to all folks, rich and poor alike. He continued to perfect his philosophy, and he also started to commit himself to writing. The writings he put together at that time were later compiled to form some of the most important writings in Confucianism, which we will cover later in more detail. He wrote poetry, details of the history of his province, and much else.

Confucius didn't exactly establish Confucianism, as we know it, or any religion or tradition for that matter. The writings he left in his last years didn't describe a new faith or system. These writings and his earlier teachings were just that — teachings. Confucianism would come about after his death with the help of those who compiled and gave new sense to his works and who believed deeply in the message Confucius was trying to get across.

After Confucius

Tomb of Philosopher Confucius in Qufu

Confucius was buried in a family tomb in his hometown after he passed away in 479 BC. Toward his final years, Confucius was probably oblivious to the impact that his wisdom would have after he had passed. In the following centuries, many scholars and philosophers who committed themselves to further developing this philosophy adopted Confucian principles.

Nonetheless, during Confucius' life and for some time after he died, his views were at odds with the popular contemporary thought. The people had lost their faiths in the traditional religious way because of a number of factors, particularly the instability and constant upheaval in China. People thus started to look elsewhere for a strong foundation of a stable society, and the pervading philosophy was one of legality. This mindset focused on strict laws, realism, and other progressive means of state-building. The ruling class saw little use in traditional rituals and old-school social conventions, and Confucius couldn't have disagreed more.

One of the first prominent philosophers who tried to carry on the torch of Confucius' teachings was Mencius (372-289 BC), also known as Mengzi or Meng Tzu.

Main Temple Building, Mencius Shrine, Shandong, China

Another important figure was Xunzi, who lived between 310 and 235 BC. Both of these philosophers agreed that Chinese society needed change, and they both saw Confucius as having provided just the right spark that China needed.

Despite having the same goal, Mengzi and Xunzi did have certain minor disagreements such as on the nature of man, for instance. As is evident from his literary contributions to Confucianism, Mengzi was a firm believer of the inherent goodness in the human heart. He believed all humanity had to do was cherish its inherent goodness. The way for people to cherish that good nature was to simply learn about Confucian philosophy and live their lives according to the wisdom. Mencius believed that the adoption of these values would make a person virtually untouchable to corruption and anything negative.

Xunzi, however, emphasized the importance of strict rituals and education to keep people in check, as he believed they were prone to corruption. In fact, his belief was that humans are likely to stray into corruption and immorality without proper guidance. That guidance came from authority and a firm commitment to education. Xunzi's goal was to keep the inherent evil at bay while Mencius believed that the goal is to cherish an already existing goodness. One of Xunzi's greatest contributions to Confucian philosophy was the writing of 32 essays, which served to give more structure and clarity to Confucianism.

During this earlier post-Confucius time, many rulers stiffly resisted his philosophy, particularly during the Qin Dynasty (221-206 BC). Confucian scholars were often targets of persecution and their writings were destroyed. Things would take a major turn for this philosophy during the reign of the Han Dynasty between 206 BC and 220 AD.

During the early Han era, other Confucian students were still introducing their own contributions after Mencius and Xunzi. Dong, who lived between 179 and 104 BC, was one example. He was a student of both prior philosophies, and he sought to combine them into one, as is evident by his belief that human nature was inherently neither good nor bad. Instead of being predetermined, one's nature was shaped later.

Still, even the early Han rulers were not exactly fond of Confucian scholars. Confucianism began to receive concrete support under Emperor Wu (141-87 BC), an important figure in the history of Confucian philosophy. Slowly but surely, the enriched and revitalized teachings of Confucius began to creep their way into matters of state, finally becoming a state doctrine before the end of the 2nd century BC.

From that point on, Confucian philosophy had the resources and the incentive to spread the word throughout China and, later, other Asian countries. For centuries, Confucianism was the core philosophy that guided both foreign and domestic policies of the Chinese Empire. Dynasties such as Song, Ming, and Qing carried the torch into the modern era. During this time, Confucianism only grew and became richer thanks to the constant reforms and contributions by the generations of scholars that came. Needless to say, all that time and effort ensured that Confucian wisdom was irreversibly embedded into Chinese tradition and mentality.

Chapter VIII:
Confucianism 101

Now that you know about the life and work of Confucius and how his philosophy came to form a religion, we will explore the ins and outs of that religion. Confucianism builds upon many ancient Chinese philosophies and philosophical concepts that are significantly older than Confucianism. One of the defining traits of Confucius' teachings is that it adds the matter of morality into the equation. Along with Taoism, Confucianism is one of the most important native philosophies of China.

The Essence of Confucianism

Confucianism stresses the importance of moral and virtuous behavior and harmony. The philosophy concerns itself with the conduct between people, which, when righteous, makes for a harmonious society. On the other hand, Confucianism also has its political teachings, which focus on the relationship between the government and its subjects. In both cases, the end goal is harmony and virtue within a society. By extension, society itself must strive to be in harmony with the Way of Heaven.

Core Teachings

Compassion between people is one of the most important goals of Confucian conduct. In fact, it's possible that the famous Golden Rule dates back to Confucius' teachings. As the *Analects* states that one should not do to others what he does not wish done to himself. Confucius' disciples put the *Analects* together as a collection of his many teachings and proverbs.

Now, while Confucianism is not exactly a god-worshiping religion, Confucius did use old Chinese religious traditions as a foundation for his philosophy. He did have a personal concept of god, but his teaching focuses primarily on earthly life and social order. People used "Tian," a traditional Chinese concept of god, for the purpose of a creator, judge, and a provider. Through Confucian life, people will be at harmony and in unity with themselves and with the divine, as will the community that the people form.

Confucius explained this harmony as being achieved through something called the Five Relationships or the Five Bonds. These common bonds make up a social structure, including parents-children, elder-younger brother, husband-wife, ruler-subjects, and friend-friend. Except for friendship, these relationships have superior and subordinate sides, taking into account patriarchal values and respect of elders. The superior side gives love, care, and guidance to the subordinate party, such as parent to child or husband to wife. According to Confucian teaching, this system of interaction is the basis for a stable and harmonious society.

Confucian Concepts

Another way to boil down the Confucian teaching is through something called the Five Constants, or the Five Virtues. These constants come together to cover all aspects of the Confucian way of life and conduct, and many things we already mentioned, such as relationships, fall under one of these virtues. They are Ren, Yi, Li, Zhi, and Xin.

Ren is essentially an encapsulation of humanity – the driving force behind everything inherently good in a person. When it comes to translation from Chinese, Ren can mean many things, such as humanness, kindness, benevolence, compassion, or altruism. Yi, or righteousness, implies self-realization and a personal orientation toward doing the right thing, a sense of morality. Li concerns rituals or, more precisely, the conduct of rituals in a proper manner and with earnest devotion.

Zhi represents wisdom and knowledge, particularly the knowledge of right and wrong. More than denoting something that should be learned from a written book, Zhi implies an innate, deep-seated sense of right and wrong. Finally, Xin is integrity, loyalty, trueness to one's word, and piety.

Scripture

When it comes to scripture, the Confucian wisdom is laid out in a variety of works that make up the Four Books and the Five Classics. Throughout the centuries and millennia, people have improved upon and added to these books. People have used Confucian writing time and time again through Chinese history to help guide people in the matters of both society and state. The Four Books include the *Great Learning*, *Analects*, *Mencius*, and the *Doctrine of the Mean*.

The Great Learning is all about morality and how one can go about cherishing and developing their moral essence. This guide encourages learning and curiosity of the world, as knowledge is seen as a way toward deeper comprehension. The *Analects* contains many of Confucius' teachings and sayings, among other things, all of which offer the reader valuable insight into the Confucian principles of morality.

Mencius is another collection that includes many of the things Confucius said and bestowed upon his learners, particularly his spiritual follower Mengzi (Mencius). The writings stress the inherent goodness of humanity, and they also touch upon matters of rule and governance. Lastly, the *Doctrine of the Mean* provides guidance on how to acquire and maintain harmony and stay on the Way. Zisi, also known as Kong Ji, who was Confucius' grandson wrote this book.

On the other hand, the Five Classics consist of the *Book of Documents, Book of Odes, Book of Rites, Book of Changes,* and the *Spring and Autumn Annals.* Invaluable pieces of Chinese literature are found within these classics, and much of the writing consists of chronicles and historical records. Works such as the *Book of Documents* detail the history and rule of numerous dynasties while others contain poetry, social analysis, social norms, moral principles, and stories of war.

Yin and Yang

The concept of Yin and Yang is something that virtually everyone has heard of, yet it is something that many don't understand. This old Chinese concept is referenced and used throughout Confucian teachings as well.

Yin and Yang can best be described as a sort of supreme, all-encompassing dichotomy or duality that, when together, results in harmony and balance. Every dichotomy that exists in this world is Yin and Yang, so to speak. Yin and Yang are thus female and male, disorder and order, winter and summer, invisible and visible, action and reaction, and so on. As you can see from some of these examples, Yin and Yang as a whole can represent many things such as humanity, history, society, the seasonal cycle, or nature itself – the totality of life on this planet.

The essence of Confucian wisdom is always somewhere along the middle way between Yin and Yang, as both are seen as complementing each other and together forming one whole.

Other Views

Being such an instructive philosophy that concerns itself so closely with matters of life on Earth, Confucianism offers a plethora of views on so many aspects of life and society. Above all, it states that our duty as human beings is to conduct ourselves with virtue and guard the wonderful planet we inhabit. Order, happiness, stability, and fulfillment are thus our responsibility, not that of a divine guardian.

Confucianism has much to say on matters that are close and known to everyone, such as marriage and death. According to Confucian teachings, the dead are buried with important possessions as well as food. The deceased's loved ones are encouraged to mourn loudly to make their loss known. The funeral itself is well-detailed as well, with instructions on how to proceed to the cemetery and organize the event.

On the other hand, marriage begins with a proposal, of course. According to custom, however, if the bride's family suffers any unfortunate incident within three days of the proposal, the marriage is canceled. Like many other religions, Confucian weddings involve gift exchanges, feasts, ceremonies, and most other things you would expect.

Confucianism in the World

For such an impactful philosophy that has left such a deep imprint on its region, Confucianism has a rather small modern base of around six million people. While individuals might practice Confucianism throughout the world, the adherents are mostly concentrated in China, Japan, South Korea, Vietnam, and Taiwan.

However, measuring the presence of Confucianism in the world by the number of people who identify as Confucians or anything of that nature is not pertinent. Not to mention, Confucianism doesn't have any order of priests or churches, as it is merely a tradition. The important thing to look at is how Confucius' philosophy helped shape societies in Asia. When we look at it like that, we quickly realize that this is one of the greatest, most important philosophies in the history of Asia.

Confucianism permeates many traditions and social norms in East Asian societies. The sense and priority of collective good, hierarchy, respect of elders, and many other things that are important in many parts of East Asia can be traced back to Confucian teachings. The orientation toward the good of the collective is particularly pronounced in many traditions throughout Asia. This mentality is quite different from some of the more individualistic cultures in the West.

None of this is surprising, of course, seeing as Confucianism has more or less been state policy in China on numerous occasions throughout history, as you have learned earlier. Just like writing systems, culture, architecture, and other influence made its way from China to early Japan, so did Confucian philosophy. Confucian principles played an important part in the reforms and social conventions of classical Japan as early as the 6th century. Shotoku Taishi, one of the earliest Japanese rulers, helped this early Chinese influence in Japan.

Furthermore, the famous samurai warriors based much of their code, also known as bushido, on the teaching of Confucius. Honor, integrity, courtesy, and self-discipline were just some of the principles that the samurai warriors held dear. In essence, the samurai were followers of the "way of the warrior," which is how "bushido" is often translated. Confucianism was implemented and reimagined in Japanese law and social order on many other occasions. Notably, this happened in the 13th century and then again in early modern Japan. Needless to say, Confucian influence is present in Japan to this day because of these historical implementations.

The Korean peninsula and the early Korean states were also under considerable Chinese influence for a long time. With the scholar Yi Hwang, Confucian teachings found a prominent place in Korea during the 16th century. Being that Confucianism is a philosophy more than an organized religion, it has always been open to interpretation and reform. This allowed for many schools of thought to emerge as the ideas spread beyond China. While Confucianism influenced different Asian societies, these societies were, in turn, influencing Confucianism.

Yi Hwang

Confucian philosophy later found itself at odds with emerging ideas that came in from the West, such as communism. This philosophical clash occurred time and time again in China. Still, rather than disappear, the teachings of ancient Confucius adapted and continued to serve their purpose in China. To this day, a strong sense of the collective good, strong family units, and aspects of education continue to carry the legacy of Confucian thought.

Conclusion

Hopefully, what you have learned in this book has given you a fresh perspective on how people around the world maintain their relationship with God or the things they believe are greater than themselves. Although they account for an enormous chunk of the world's religious folks, the four religions we have explored merely scratch the surface of the intricacies of human worship and philosophy.

If you can think of a way for people to pray and worship, the chances are good that it's been done already. So many religions are still practiced to this day that it would be next to impossible to study all of them in one lifetime. In fact, it's estimated that there could be as many as 4,200 religions being practiced today, which is a lot of gods and even more rituals and customs.

Of course, you now understand that religion is often much more than praying and worshiping any god. It's a way to live and find harmony in life, not just with others but with ourselves. Most civilizations in the world, with all their norms, conventions, morals, and even hierarchy were built or at least reinforced by their respective religions.

Understanding other religions is a great way to bridge the gap between those different cultures and understand more about them. More often than not, we find that despite all the differences in practice and teaching, the majority of our diverse world's faiths work toward the same common goals at their very essence. As such, religion can be a common tongue and a way to demonstrate that we're not all that different.

That's why learning is important, and you have now hopefully acquired just enough knowledge to understand where other cultures are coming from. At the very least, it is the author's hope to have sparked in you a desire to learn even more about our fascinating world and to never stop learning about and trying to understand other people.

More from Us

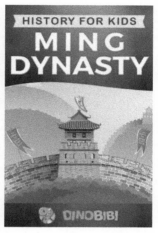

CPSIA information can be obtained
at www.ICGtesting.com
Printed in the USA
BVHW032002110123
656099BV00001B/18

9 781076 369284